SHISHA
EMBROIDERY
Traditional Indian Mirror Work with Instructions and Transfer Patterns

Nancy D. Gross & Frank Fontana

Dover Publications, Inc.
New York

Acknowledgments

We would like to thank several people in particular, without whose enthusiastic cooperation this book would have been more difficult to write and less interesting to read—Judy Dillon, of Madison, Wisconsin, whose slides, maps and diagrams of Sindhi embroidery filled in some large gaps; Mrs. Jerry Zarbaugh, of Aardvark Adventures in Handcrafts, whose correspondence contained many illuminating reflections; Jean Simpson, of Kitsophrenia, Inc., whose response to our inquiries was most generous; Betty Tyres, of the India Study Room, Victoria & Albert Museum, London, for allowing access to their priceless textile collection; and our editor, Rita Weiss.

To my parents, Fred and Anita,
my sister Wendy, IKA,
and the late Monty.
—N.D.G.

To Mom and Dad.
—F.F.

Published in Canada by General Publishing Company, Ltd., 30 Lesmill Road, Don Mills, Toronto, Ontario.
Published in the United Kingdom by Constable and Company, Ltd., 10 Orange Street, London WC2H 7EG.

Shisha Embroidery: Traditional Indian Mirror Work with Instructions and Transfer Patterns is a new work, first published by Dover Publications, Inc., in 1981.

International Standard Book Number: 0-486-24043-6
Library of Congress Catalog Card Number: 80-69676

Manufactured in the United States of America
Dover Publications, Inc.
31 East 2nd Street
Mineola N.Y. 11501.

Introduction

India, Pakistan, Afghanistan—the mere mention of these countries conjures up images of magnificent temples, mosques and ruins, high mountains, burning deserts and tropical jungles, and people dressed in intensely colorful turbans, graceful lengths of saris and deftly embroidered garments. Although now separate political units, these three countries have been considered parts of a single social and political entity through much of recorded history, thus sharing many traits especially in the area of folk art. One of the folk arts in which this age-old continuity is most evident is the form of traditional Indian embroidery called *shisha,* or *mirrorwork.*

In ancient times, professional embroiderers and their wealthy clients could afford to have their garments decorated with the most costly of precious jewels and metallic threads. But this privileged class has always made up a very small segment of India's population.

The less prosperous classes, still desiring some glamour and glitter in their otherwise drab lives, were forced to resort to more practical and cheaper decorative materials. Originally, silvery beetles' wings and small chips of mica were embroidered onto cloth to give the fabrics a rich and luxurious look. Later, during Moghul times (c. 1500-1850), a process was developed for manufacturing tiny mirror discs from sand, lime and soda in small furnaces. These miniature mirrors were immediately adopted by artisans for all sorts of decorative purposes. They were called *shisha,* which actually means "glass" or "mirror" in Hindustani.

Embroiderers began to attach these rough mirrors with a framework of stitches to all sorts of everyday garments, ceremonial textiles and ornamental trappings. Mumtaz Mahal, the wife of the great Moghul emperor Shah Jahan, is credited by some with having originated the idea and techniques for shisha embroidery. Her husband was a prodigious builder who also incorporated entire rooms of mirror mosaics into his palatial fortresses at Lahore in Pakistan, and Delhi and Agra in India. These rooms were called *shish mahals,* "palaces of mirrors," and can still be seen today. This architectural motif has been revived recently in India, and one can stay in first-class tourist hotels whose lobbies and restaurants are modern *shish mahals.*

Mumtaz Mahal died while giving birth to their fourteenth child in 1631. Shah Jahan was so grief-stricken by this sudden loss that he initiated his most ambitious architectural project—a mausoleum in which they could lie side-by-side for all eternity—the *Taj Mahal.* But, sadly, Shah Jahan was denied his final wish. His son, Aurangzeb, overthrew him in 1658 and imprisoned Shah Jahan in his own fort in Agra, directly across the Jumna River from the Taj Mahal. The cruelest irony of all was that, until his death eight years later, he was not permitted to gaze directly at the tomb of his beloved wife. He was forced to look only on its reflection in a small *shisha* embedded in a pillar of the fort which faced the Taj. In the end, the mirrors which he and his wife had used to enrich the embroidery and architecture of an entire empire formed the last link between the two ill-fated lovers.

Unlike other Indian embroidery forms where traditional motifs and color schemes were modified to suit the changing tastes of those Indians who adopted foreign styles and of those foreigners living and working in India and to cater to rapidly expanding foreign markets, shisha embroidery has remained basically unchanged in ancient techniques, symbolic motifs and ritually determined color schemes. Shisha embroidery is part of the great tradition of domestic embroidery practiced in the home by women who were taught embroidery by their mothers, aunts and older sisters as soon as their tiny fingers could grasp the needle. Not subject to the whims of fashion, isolated from the outside world, these women created beautiful embroidered pieces which are at once unique works of art and treasure troves of a craft heritage which has continued unbroken for almost five thousand years.

Shisha embroidery done today by the women of the rural and traditional segments of Indian, Pakistani and Afghan society is one of the last holdouts against modernization and Western influence.

For the rural, pastoral and nomadic women of these regions, shisha embroidery is a major folk activity. Their way of life is dependent on the weather and the seasons for planting and harvesting, grazing and herding, and other traditional occupations. During the long periods of time between chores, the women work on elaborate shisha embroideries. The brilliant mirrors, the bright colors and the bold motifs serve to reflect and enhance their everyday lives.

The most prevalent and widespread motifs seem to date back to the beginnings of Indian civilization. The stylized plants and animals are executed in primitive fashion, with no pretense of perspective or shadow. Geometric designs are often divided into groups of three or its multiples. Vegetable motifs of creeping vines, trees of life, lotuses, mangos and flower buds reflect the ancient preoccupation with the fertility of crops, livestock and women. The animal motifs of peacocks, parrots, elephants and cattle echo those concerns.

The traditional colors speak of an elemental lifestyle, in harmony with nature, the seasons and the inevitable processes of birth, youth, aging and death. Red is the color of youth, passion and marriage. Saffron yellow is the color of spring, and indigo blue of the clouded sky during the rainy season, a time for romance and longing. Maroon and black are the colors of mourning, white indicates purity and high spirituality.

This book contains complete instructions for working this embroidery technique plus 24 embroidery transfer patterns, based upon actual examples of shisha embroidery, which are shown in the color photographs on the covers. The transfer pattern plates have been rendered in such a way as to preserve the groupings and spacing of the motifs in the authentic pieces of embroidery. If you wish to try and recreate some of the traditional wall hangings and other pieces from which these designs are taken, you can arrange the plates in similar positions and use them as they are.

If you do not wish to recreate the traditional pieces pictured here, there are many other ways in which you can use these motifs. Any single design may be cut out and used separately, as a central motif on a project. Designs from different plates may be cut out and worked on a single piece, preserving the traditional feeling of shisha embroidery while reflecting your own taste and individual preferences. The combinations are endless.

Individual motifs or groups of designs may be transferred to cloth and made up into many attractive and practical items. Most popular are: the yokes and sleeves of blouses, the panels and straps of shoulder and tote bags, placemats and napkins, tablecloths, throw-pillow and cushion covers, tee shirts, drawstring purses, and wall hangings. These are just a few of the articles that lend themselves to shisha embroidery. In time, you'll discover others that seem made just for this sort of flashy yet tasteful ethnic embroidery.

The Regional Styles of Shisha Embroidery

Shisha embroidery is done in a vast, contiguous region of southwestern Asia and the northwestern part of the Indian subcontinent. This area stretches from the windswept, desolate mountains of Afghanistan, through the steppes and deserts of Baluchistan and the coastal and alluvial plains of Sindh in Pakistan, to the harsh wastes of Kuch, the pleasant, fertile hills of Kathiawar, and the rugged, isolated highlands of the Deccan plateau in India. Within this area, there are several regional styles of shisha embroidery. Often each tribal or ethnic group within a particular region has its own unique style, techniques and use for shisha embroideries. Traditional distinctions between groups can be traced in the staunchly individual garments and decorations, embroidered with mirrors, beads and spangles in characteristic fashion.

AFGHAN SHISHA EMBROIDERY

Shisha embroidery in Afghanistan is done by both men and women. Silk or cotton thread is used to embroider the designs on a ground of cotton, sheepskin or leather. Everyday articles, such as men's skullcaps, prayer mats, cushion covers, long dresses, blouses, coats and wallets are worked in shisha embroidery. Ceremonial objects such as saddles and bridles for horse fairs, and cloths for wrapping copies of the holy Quran, the sacred book of the Muslims, are intricately decorated with fine shisha work.

The motifs used in Afghan embroidery are highly abstract and geometric. People are very rarely depicted because of the Islamic injunction against making idols which, when strictly interpreted, forbids any sort of realistic representation. Popular motifs include arches and domes from mosques, stars, diamonds, triangles, leaves, vines and flowers. A hand is often incorporated into shisha embroideries to ward off the evil eye.

Shisha work from Kandahar in south-central Afghanistan is characterized by mirrors surrounded with areas of very heavy embroidery. The work done by the women from the various Pathan tribes in eastern Afghanistan uses mirrors as the centers of concentric rows of stitched beadwork called *guls*, or roses. These *guls* are then attached as a single unit to the cloth or garment to be decorated.

The embroidery which accompanies and accentuates the mirrorwork is done in a number of stitches. Tent and satin stitch are the most popular for filling and outlining. Other stitches include backstitch, cross stitch, stem stitch, straight stitch and couched work. Recently, embroidery has been developed as a craft for export, and much of the work produced for foreign trade is done by inferior machine stitching.

PAKISTANI SHISHA EMBROIDERY

Many intricate styles of folk embroidery are practiced by women throughout Pakistan. Shisha embroidery is the specialty of the women of the Baluchistan and Sindh provinces. The strong Islamic traditions of these people are evident in the use of predominantly geometric and abstract shisha embroidery motifs. Stylized floral designs take their inspiration from the world-famous Gardens of Shalimar and *shish mahal* in Lahore, where the Moghuls' loving use of flowers and mirrored mosaics are echoed in the humbler but no less exquisite creations of traditional shisha embroiderers.

Baluchistan, so close geographically to Muslim Iran and Afghanistan, produces almost purely geometric shisha embroideries. Sindh, on the other hand, is adjacent to Hindu areas of India such as Gujarat, and has been subject to a combination of Islamic and Hindu influences over the centuries. There was always a free exchange of ideas, culture and population between the two states until 1947, when the separate countries of India and Pakistan were formed. Thus, there are traces of Hindu motifs, color schemes and stitches in Sindhi shisha embroidery. In general appearance, Sin-

NORTH-WEST
FRONTIER
PROVINCE

JAMMU
& KASHMIR

KANDAHAR

● Islamabad

PUNJAB

BALUCHISTAN

HARYANA

New Delhi ●

UTTAR
PRADESH

RAJASTHAN

SINDH

BIHAR

● Bhuj

GUJARAT

MADHYA PRADESH

BENGAL

DECCAN PLATEAU

ORISSA

MAHARASHTRA

ANDHRA PRADESH

KARNATAKA

TAMIL
NADU

KERALA

MAP OF INDIA
Showing Places Mentioned in the Text

dhi shisha work is much closer to that of Gujarat than to Baluchi embroidery.

Baluchi Shisha Embroidery

The Baluchis are a pastoral and nomadic people who spend much of the year herding their sheep and goats to sparse grazing land up and down the mountains and plains of southern Afghanistan, western Pakistan and eastern Iran. Shisha embroidery has been practiced by Baluchi women for several centuries.

Traditional shisha embroidery is used to decorate the everyday clothes of women and children, and also to enhance the beauty of the holiday clothing worn at weddings and the livestock fairs, races and wrestling competitions that the Baluchis are so fond of. The most famous shisha pieces from Baluchistan are the *pushk kurtas,* calf-length blouses for women made of satin. These *kurtas* have densely embroidered fronts containing mirrors surrounded by bands of geometric patterns worked so closely the ground fabric is no longer visible. The center of the blouse features a long, rectangular pocket ending in a triangular point; it is unique to Baluchi shisha blouses. The cuffs at the end of the long sleeves are worked in matching motifs.

Older shisha embroidery is notable for its use of natural dyes which result in subdued, almost muted color schemes. Modern shisha work is produced largely at government training centers located near the provincial capital of Quetta. (Plate 24 is taken from a modern *kurta* made in Quetta.) These centers instruct young women and girls in the art of shisha embroidery, preserving a traditional craft and, at the same time, providing them with a steady source of income. Modern work is geared primarily towards the tourist and export trades, and features untraditionally loud colors such as hot pink, lemon yellow, sky blue and chartreuse. The most popular motifs are flowers with shishas at the center of a series of geometric or triangular petals. The designs cover large areas and are often outlined in black backstitch and filled with long satin stitch. Those sections not completely covered with embroidery are filled with seed stitches, detached chain stitches, or French knots.

Baluchi shisha work is done with cotton thread on heavy cotton material. Square pieces of shisha embroidery are often sold unmounted to be made up into shirt fronts, shoulder bags, tea cozies and pillow covers. More recently, Baluchistan has begun to export cotton knit tee shirts embroidered with simple shisha designs. These shirts have become quite fashionable and can be seen all over the world. One hopes that government embroidery schools will preserve the true heritage of Baluchi embroidery, which is dying out, along with introducing new and appreciative audiences to the more commercial shisha pieces.

Sindhi Shisha Embroidery

Sindh lies on a plain between the Arabian Sea and the headwaters of the Indus River, the birthplace of Indian civilization and cotton cultivation. The people of Sindh have always excelled in textile arts. In addition to the heritage passed down from the Indus Valley culture, Sindh has been subject to continuous outside influences and ties with its neighboring Hindu and Muslim states. Due to these factors, Sindhi shisha work is probably the most complex of the regional styles.

Sindh is famous for all of its embroidery, and the most characteristic shisha work combines as many as six or seven embroidery techniques on cloth that has been elaborately prepared in advance, using a wide variety of stitches and motifs which bear traces of the relative harmony of Muslim and Hindu cultures in Sindh until recent times.

Shisha embroidery is done on a cotton ground which is resist dyed or block printed before the actual needlework begins. Long strips of material are joined together to form the multicolored ground cloth. Many women bring this cloth to the *chapagar,* the woodblock printer, who works out of a small stall in the bazaar of every village. The women pick out whichever motifs they wish to embroider and the *chapagar* stamps the outlines on the fabric with carved wooden blocks. According to the plan of the needleworker, he distributes these patterns evenly over the entire piece, or groups them around larger motifs already dyed into the cloth. Some women even keep a small set of their favorite motifs at home and print their fabrics themselves.

Once the ground cloth has been prepared, the shishas are attached with the needlework frame to parts of the motif for emphasis. Then, embroidery is worked in cotton or silk floss around these mirrors. The distinctive interlacing stitches and Maltese crosses for fillings, and the ladder stitches, chain and open chain stitches for borders and flowers give Sindhi shisha work its characteristic look. Truly unique is the combination of mirrorwork with large areas of counted cross stitch. A type of darning stitch, borrowed from Panjabi embroidery known as *phulkari,* is also used to cover large areas. French knots and star stitches fill in the open sections of the work. Stem stitch and backstitch are used for the outlines, often worked in black and white thread, as in Baluchi embroidery.

The most popular motifs and color schemes in Sindhi shisha embroidery are drawn from many sources. Triangular, trefoil and tripartite designs are everywhere. These can be traced back to the embroiderers of the Indus Valley culture. Mango, parrot, peacock and lotus motifs bear the naturalistic traces of Hindu influence. The floral and delicate geometric motifs reflect the more dominant Islamic preference for repetition and infinite variation.

Many of the motifs used have superstitious origins. The paisley, spiral, disc and peacock feather designs are considered symbols of the life-giving power of the sun. These were embroidered on precious garments to avert the evil eye, which was brought on by the gaze of jealous admirers. As a final safeguard, the shisha mirrors would deflect the glance of the ill-wisher, and return the curse to its originator.

In northern Sindh, the motifs are more abstract, and the mellower color schemes echo those of Baluchistan and Afghanistan. In the south, which is more renowned for shisha work, the colors are more garish and the featured motifs are stylized yet recognizable representations of animals, men and women because of the Gujarati influence. Of all the tribes in southern Sindh famed for their skill in embroidery, none is more highly regarded than the *Mochi*, who were originally cobblers and who are credited with developing the most sophisticated techniques in shisha embroidery over three hundred years ago.

There are a number of typical garments embroidered by Sindhi women that feature shisha work. Many of these pieces figure prominently in wedding ceremonies. As soon as a daughter is born, her female relatives begin work on a *guj*, or wedding tunic worn by Muslim women of western Sindh. Just before the wedding, the completed *guj*, encrusted with shisha work and silk embroidery, is presented to the bride. During the course of the ceremony, the bride wears the *guj* with the neck slit in the back. After her first night with her new husband, she turns the *guj* around and wears the slit facing front. To insure a long and happy marriage, the *guj* is worn constantly until it becomes threadbare and falls apart. The groom at the ceremony wears a *bokhani*, a wedding scarf which is draped over his shoulders. The ground is red or white cotton with shisha embroidery of chain, stem, interlacing and ladder stitch and couching worked in silk floss. Animal motifs, such as peacocks, camels, elephants and scorpions point to the Hindu origin of this traditional trapping. Also called a *bhet*, the scarf can be wrapped around a turban or worn as a sash. Plates 21, 22 and 23 are adapted from these scarfs. A *malir* is a man's wedding shawl, done on blockprinted red and black cloth called *ajrak*. The four corners of this large shawl are heavily worked in circular shisha and peacock motifs with silk floss. A similar everyday garment for men, called a *chadar*, has less elaborate shisha work. The woman has her own bridal shawl, worn on special occasions and a necessary part of her dowry, called an *abbocchnai*. Shisha and silk floss are carefully and delicately worked along with counted cross stitch and interlacing on a red or white cotton ground. Long, bulky wedding skirts worn by the Hindu brides of Sindh are called *paros*. These skirts of rust-colored handloomed cotton virtually explode with bursts of shisha-worked peacocks, flowers, vines, buds, spiral whorls and sun discs. Due to the shift in Hindu and Muslim populations in 1947, these skirts are no longer produced in Sindh but similar ones can be found in Gujarat.

Sindhi women adorn everyday objects, as well, with shisha work. Children's clothes, skullcaps, blankets, wallhangings, Quran covers, prayer mats, and shirts and trousers are given as much attention as pieces for weddings. Much shisha embroidery is now done for the tourist and export trade, producing pieces such as pillow covers, tea cozies, shoulder bags and blouses. Even in the face of this commercialization, Sindhi embroidery manages to retain its unique style and flavor.

INDIAN SHISHA EMBROIDERY

India is an ancient, vast and densely populated country containing many ethnic, religious and language groups and innumerable castes, tribes, clans and occupational subgroups. The diversity of all folk crafts—including embroidery—in India is equalled perhaps nowhere in the world. While different styles and types of embroidery are done in all parts of India, the northwestern province of Gujarat has, over the centuries, earned a reputation for producing some of the best commercial and traditional embroidered articles in the world.

Generally, the shisha work of Gujarat is highly representational, depicting in primitive style the exploits of Hindu gods, heroes, kings, princes, battles, and tragic love stories. Motifs of elephants, chariots, horses, soldiers, and princes or couples on palanquins tell the traditional stories. Although the patterns for the flower motifs, *butas*, and the buds, *butis*, are sometimes stamped with woodblocks, the animal and human figures are always drawn by hand.

Traditional Gujarati homes are festooned with shisha embroidery. Shisha hangings decorate beams, doorways, walls, corner niches, shelves and beds. Women's skirts and bodices are adorned with mirrors, as are children's caps and gowns. During festivals, cattle are weighed down with heavily embroidered shisha trappings, each piece having a special name and ritual meaning.

Even among the fabled embroiderers of Gujarat, there are certain tribes which are considered outstanding craftspeople. These are the tribes living in Kuch and Kathiawar, two regions also famed for the chain stitch.

Shisha embroidery is the specialty of the women of Kuch and Kathiawar, almost all of whom have learned to embroider by the early teens. The shisha work they do greatly resembles that of neighboring Sindh. The motifs and techniques all seem to have their origins in the pastoral, nomadic way of life which must have been the lot of their common ancestors. The shared motifs of mangoes, parrots, peacocks, elephants, lotus flowers, vines and buds, show the exchange of traditional ideas which has taken place between the people of this area over the years. There are noticeable differences, however, particularly in the styles of the individual tribes.

Kuchi Shisha Embroidery

Kuch is a sandy, desolate peninsula in the state of Gujarat. In spite of its forbidding terrain, the flat wastes have invited numerous invasions, one in the thirteenth century, and another in the eighteenth from Sindh, that have left a substantial minority of the people Muslims. The majority of the nomadic and tribal people, however, are Hindu. According to legend, the art of shisha embroidery was first introduced to the *Mochis*, cobblers, of Kuch by a Muslim holy man from Sindh in the seventeenth century.

Kuch is the major center for the production of a type of shisha work in which chain stitch predominates. Although any piece of shisha embroidery is sometimes mistakenly termed Kuch work, authentic Kuch work always features chain stitch worked with a hook called an *ari*. The *ari* is a smaller version of a shoemaker's awl and attests to the historical link between the two crafts. Use of the *ari* permits the Kuchi embroiderer to execute her motifs with a speed, neatness and precision unequalled in the other types of shisha embroidery. It is by this polished and sophisticated look that true Kuch work can be recognized. Other common stitches, such as herringbone, closed herringbone, stem, couching, darning, satin and ladder, are worked by hand on the ground of homespun cotton with a floss of silk, cotton or, more rarely, wool.

The mirrors, which are called *abhala*, and metallic spangles called *tiki* are embroidered onto skirts, bodices, door and wall hangings, quilt covers, children's clothes, and cattle trappings.

The most popular motifs also show the traces of pastoral life. Bulls, cows, oxcarts and milkmaids all appear in characteristically wide, flat designs. The floral and vine motifs, *butas*, are more natural and less angular than those of Sindh, while the figures are more easily recognized as people.

A very distinctive set of motifs appears in Kuchi embroidery which is found in no other school. Due to the advanced nature of Kuchi embroidery, the patronage of local princes extended itself to the humble art of needlework and many wall hangings were commissioned by petty rajahs. In order to recreate the pomp and pageantry of these regional courts, the embroiderers produced scenes overflowing with processions of princes and their wives and concubines on palanquins beneath splendid canopies and peacock fans; soldiers, royally caparisoned elephants, camels, horses and attendants surrounded them. Hindu religious symbols such as swastikas and the sun and the moon are also common.

The styles and purposes of Kuch embroidery vary from region to region and tribe to tribe. There are a large number of different groups, some of the more important of which are discussed below. The *Mochi*, who live around the provincial capital of Bhuj, are the most famous for producing top-quality shisha embroidery. The hook-worked chain stitch surrounds the mirrors and fills out the motifs in tightly executed concentric rows. This type of work has even been named after the tribe and is referred to as *mochi bharat*. It is used to decorate an exquisite garment known as a *ghaghra*, a skirt made of satin and densely worked along the hem with several borders, and veritable jungles of flowers and parrots covering the rest of the fabric.

Another style is *kanbi*, done mostly by peasant women and cowherds of the *Kanbi* and *Ahir* tribes. *Kanbi* embroidery was brought up from the south and shows its nomadic Kathiawari origins in the use of bright orange, yellow or white ground for motifs of sunflowers, parakeets, roundels and octagons done in handworked chain stitch, satin stitch and herringbone stitch.

The *Jats* of northern Kuch trace their ancestors back to Baluchistan and the shisha embroidery they produce seems to bear this out. Work is done on rough homespun cotton of indigo, green or other subdued colors. The abstract and finely worked geometric patterns of antique Baluchi embroidery are indeed typical of the *Jat* shisha work, but the very generous use of mirrors and the naturalistic portrayal of plants and flowers are local adaptations. The greater variety of stitches used is also due to Kuchi influence. Chain, running, straight, and closed herringbone stitches are common. A typical piece of clothing, called an *aba*, is a long, mirrorworked tunic which is worn over baggy pants, *salwar*, by *Jat* women. The shisha embroidery on the blouse is done in several colors of silk floss on a cotton fabric. Those parts of the trousers which are visible beneath the *aba* are also elaborately embroidered. Plate 19 is adapted from an *aba*.

The *Lohanas*, neighbors of the *Jats*, settled in Kuch after fleeing Sindh some two centuries ago. Their shisha embroidery echoes that of their ancestral home-land in its use of open chain and ladder stitch on maroon-colored cotton ground with multicolored silk floss. A distinctive *Lohana* motif is an eight-sided figure filled in with stylized flowers, buds, and vines. Women's skirts, blankets, sleeveless tops called *cholis*, and long-sleeved blouses for unmarried women called *ungias*, are lovingly covered with shisha work and chain-stitch embroidery by the women of Kuch. Plate 18 is taken from an embroidered piece worked by *Lohana* embroiderers in Kuch.

Kathiawari Shisha Embroidery

Kathiawar is a prosperous Gujarati region famous for its high-quality cotton crop and textile factories. Prize and pampered milk cows also make their home there. Over the centuries, the favorable conditions of Kathi-awar have attracted farmers, herders, artisans, and holy men from the less hospitable lands of Kuch and Sindh. It should come as no surprise that the shisha work of Kathiawar shares many common traits with that of those two regions.

Kathiawari embroidery makes the same lavish use of mirrors, bright colors and wide variety of stitches as Kuch work. The most popular stitches are satin, darn-ing, herringbone, closed herringbone and hand-worked chain. Unlike Kuchi embroidery, the very long satin or darning stitch is used to fill large squares and triangle motifs, rather than compact chain stitch in curved or circular designs. It is said that the renowned *Mochi* embroiderers of Kuch, in search of greener pas-tures and wealthy clients, emigrated to Kathiawar towards the end of the nineteenth century. While they retained many of the floral and royal motifs, they abandoned the use of the tiny chain stitch for filling in favor of the quicker, easier satin or darning stitch. While the *Mochi* embroiderers still managed to pro-duce elegant shisha pieces in silk chain stitch worked on silk ground for rich and ostentatious landlords, they incorporated local stitches and rustic motifs into much of their everyday shisha embroidery. There are still workshops of *Mochi* embroiderers in Kathiawar, but they work in inferior styles using sewing machines to do once-handcrafted pieces.

Native Kathiawari work is most often done by pea-sant women on a cotton ground with silk or cotton floss. The predominant stitch is the long satin stitch for filling, with stem stitch or couching outlining the designs. While Kathiawari motifs include the obliga-tory Hindu scenes of gods, kings and heroes, rural life and its everyday motifs are also given full attention. Cows, bulls, horns, tails and hooves become abstract, decorative details. There is a greater spontaneity and life in the human, animal and plant figures due to the freer application of needlework stitches and the prac-tice of drawing the designs individually by hand. An-other idiosyncrasy of Kathiawari shisha embroidery is the custom of leaving a small corner of the piece unfin-ished. This is to ward off the evil eye, which could be fatal if the envy of an admirer were aroused by a com-plete, and therefore perfect, piece of work.

There are some notable regional and ethnic varieties of shisha embroidery within Kathiawar. The immigrant *Mochis*, mentioned above, were, in fact, encouraged to come by the *Kathis*, the elite land-owning class who were esteemed as the best embroiderers of Kathiawar during the nineteenth century. With the advent of the *Mochis*, the *Kathis* could afford to pay for the tedious and time-consuming shisha work done by others, and they gradually lost the skills and traditions to carry on the craft themselves. The *Mahajans* are a class of mer-chants and traders from the southwest whose women produce a unique style of shisha embroidery which features large squares divided into four or nine smaller squares, each filled with long satin stitches of a single color, most often purple, blue or red. The mirrors are lined up in straight rows along the borders and inter-sections. Outer borders are worked in checkerboard and triangle designs. The *Mahajans* use some chain and herringbone stitches for outlines and filling in borders. They now use machine-made cloth for the ground. The *Kanbis* of Kathiawar take their bold and primitive motifs from their everyday rural life, and transform mundane animals, people and objects into glittering motifs worked on intensely colored orange or yellow cloth in multicolored threads.

The women of Kathiawar embroider just about any-thing they can get their hands on. Each piece of shisha work has its precise name and exact function. A *nati* is a cap for young boys which resembles the hat worn by French foreign legionaires, with a long flap in the back. The flap protects the precious male offspring from the ill effects of the sun while he plays among the cows or in the fields. There is no such cap for young daugh-ters. A *toran* is a hanging which frames the doorway and symbolizes the hospitality and warmth of the Gu-jarati household. *Pachhitpatis* are narrow strips of shisha work that are hung along the tops of the walls. They stretch out to depict divine and royal parades, parties and battles. *Pattis* are smaller versions which hang from the edges of storage shelves. These pieces are derived from the stone carvings which were archi-tectural accents on the ancient Hindu temples. The in-genuity of the traditional embroiderers has translated these classic motifs and forms into a lively and every-day art.

A *chakla* is a square piece of shisha work which is used to wrap the bride's dowry and wedding outfit.

After the marriage, these *chaklas* are hung on the walls of the newlyweds' bedroom, to insure a happy and productive union. *Chaklas* and *pacchitpatis* are joined together by strips of patchwork applique to form very large hangings called *bhitiyas*. These are brought out only on special occasions and are displayed outside the house. Another type of large wall hanging called an *ochhad* is used to decorate the walls inside the house. The mirrors and embroidered designs usually focus around a central, circular motif which represents the sun. Animals, parrots, heroes, and flowers in pairs or groups decorate the rest of the piece. Multiple borders which have been embroidered with mirrors and abstract motifs separately are appliqued around the edges to complete the *ochhad*. Plates 1-15 are adapted from an *ochhad* from Kathiawar. *Sthapanas* are small shisha pieces depicting a god, used to decorate the family shrine (see plates 16 and 17). There are a vast number of shisha articles for every purpose one can imagine. Even the trappings for cattle have individual names, depending on whether the piece fits over the horn, the back, the tail or the head of the animal. The attention showered by the Kathiawari men on their livestock at festival time is second only to the attention and care paid by Kathiawari women to their shisha embroidery.

Nomadic Shisha Embroidery

Central India is inhabited by tribes of nomads who have maintained a strong tradition of shisha embroidery. Due to their seasonal shifts, it is difficult to pinpoint these people, but they wander through an area that includes Gujarat, southern Rajasthan and the Deccan plateau. Some researchers believe that the practice of attaching mirrors, beads and shells to fabric with stitches actually originated among these tribes, and then spread to the other inhabitants of Kathiawar, Kuch and Sindh.

Similarities in the motifs, techniques and kinds of shisha pieces certainly do exist, but it is difficult to determine how and where this method of embroidery began. A major difference in nomadic work is the heavy use of many large and irregularly shaped shishas. Very often, no ground cloth at all is left showing, and there is no room for decorative embroidery on the garment. Only the round, square, oval and triangular mirrors and their stitched frameworks are visible. Mirrors of many different shapes and sizes are often combined on a single garment.

The two major tribes known for their shisha embroidery are the *Banjaras* and the *Rabaris*. The *Banjaras* roam the Deccan plateau with their flocks. Their women embroider on a ground of handloomed cotton strips joined together, using satin and herringbone stitches worked in cotton floss. The *Rabari* tribes move primarily through Kuch. In addition to the common herringbone and satin stitches, they work in cross stitch and double cross stitch on a ground of maroon or black cotton.

The *Banjaras, Rabaris* and other tribes have no permanent houses. Therefore they do not waste their time embroidering household decorations, like their more settled neighbors. Tents, blankets, quilts and other portable articles more suited to their travels are done in shisha embroidery. The most elaborate work, however, is reserved for garments. Each tribe's use of mirrors, motifs and color schemes is so distinctive, that members of a particular tribe can be identified merely by the outfits they wear. The nomadic women wear heavily gathered skirts, brief halters and tie-dyed shawls decorated with shisha work. The men dress much more simply, with perhaps just a touch of color and glimmer of mirrors in cloths wrapped into their turbans. The children, especially the pampered baby boys, are sometimes dressed only in a mirrored shirt and a tiny mirrored bonnet. Just as these isolated tribes have struggled to preserve their traditional way of life, so have the nomadic women preserved an older form of shisha embroidery which is unique in its beauty and simplicity.

How to Do Shisha Embroidery

FABRICS

In the past, shisha embroidery was worked on hand-loomed cotton or silk ground or, very occasionally, on thin, coarse wool. The cloth was of solid colors from natural dyes, which gave the finished pieces a warm, rich glow. The one exception to the use of a single color for the ground material was in Sindhi work, where the hand-dyed, tie-dyed or woodblock-printed fabrics set up a subtle contrast to the embroidered shisha designs. The modern shisha embroidery done for sale and export has expanded the range of materials. *Kurtas* (see plate 24) from Sindh and Baluchistan are now worked on satin and shiny rayon which resembles silk. Flat crepe is also used for fancy shisha embroidery on dressy blouses. Readymade cotton-knit tee shirts provide a versatile and lighthearted background to simple shisha designs. And for small decorative pieces which tourists often buy as souvenirs of local handicrafts, such as purses, wallets and tea cozies, mirrorwork is often done on velvet along with appliquéd gold braid and embellishments stitched in metallic threads.

Some kinds of fabric are more suited to shisha embroidery than others. The material you choose should be substantial enough to support the weight of the mirrors and heavy embroidery. The texture, feel and look of the fabric can reinforce and harmonize with the effect of what is essentially a rustic and robust embroidery technique, although with a carefully thought-out color scheme, the overall impression of your shisha work can be extremely smart and sophisticated. Avoid thin and sheer fabrics, double knits and other synthetics which may stretch too much. Medium-weight cottons and cotton-polyester blends are ideal grounds for shisha embroidery. A natural choice would be handloomed cottons of various colors and weaves which are imported from India and Pakistan. For an eclectic but still ethnic look, handloomed cottons from Central and South America, in numerous solids and striped patterns, are interesting choices and are generally available. Closely woven linen is also suitable.

There are really no hard-and-fast rules for selecting the best type of material with the proper color and texture for the unique shisha project you have in mind. One of the creative challenges of working in shisha embroidery is combining all the diverse elements into a finished piece of needle art. One thing to keep in mind, however, particularly when using handloomed and hand-dyed cotton fabrics, is that the material should be washed before any embroidery is begun, to allow for shrinkage and the running of colors.

MIRRORS

The traditional shisha mirrors manufactured in Gujarat and Pakistan are roughly circular, silver in color with an irregular, bubbly texture. Mirrors also come in pale green, blue and gold, but these are much less common, since the blast furnaces must be thoroughly cleaned before and after manufacturing each color. Formerly, practically every village in the regions where shisha embroidery is done had its own small shisha factory where the mirrors were produced by hand. Gujarati factories even exported mirrors to Sindh, Baluchistan and Afghanistan. Now there is only one major shisha factory in operation in India and several in Pakistan. Some of these mirrors are exported and can be obtained from needlework shops or from the sources listed at the end of this book. Still, the output of these factories is not enough to satisfy the demand of embroiderers, and recently mass-produced mirrors from Eastern Europe have been imported into Pakistan and India to be incorporated along with traditional techniques, stitches and motifs.

It is best to use the actual imported mirrors made specifically for shisha embroidery. Nothing can match them for durability and washability; they are thin and light yet easy to work with and incredibly tough. Garments embroidered with genuine shisha can be washed repeatedly by hand or machine with no ill effects if the framework of stitches has been worked

Instructions continue following transfer patterns.

Test Pattern

PLATE 1

Test Pattern

PLATE 1

PLATE 2

Test Pattern

PLATE 2

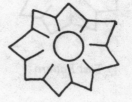

Test Pattern

PLATE 3

Test Pattern

PLATE 3

Test Pattern

PLATE 4

Test Pattern

PLATE 4

Test Pattern

PLATE 5

Test Pattern

PLATE 5

PLATE 9

PLATE 6

PLATE 7

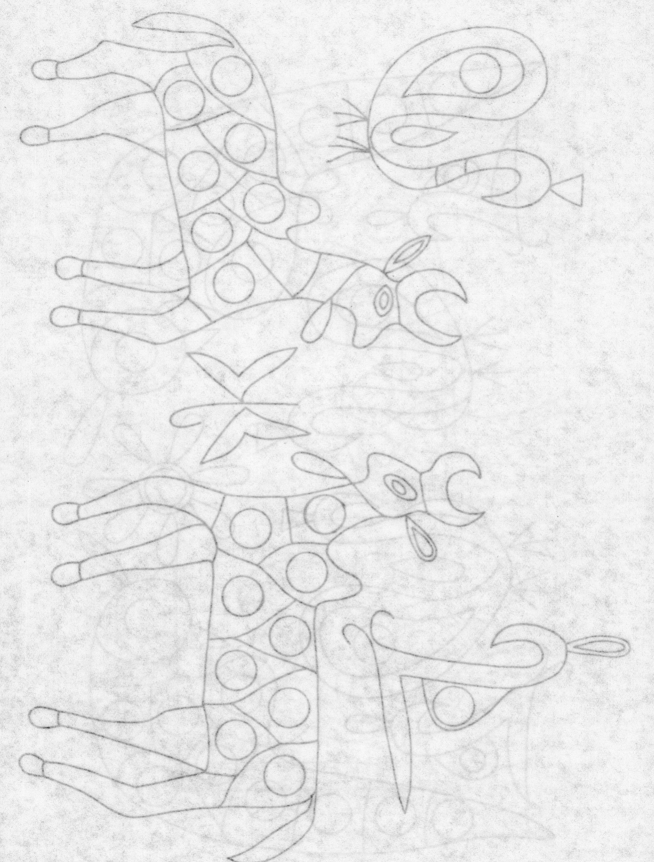

PLATE 8

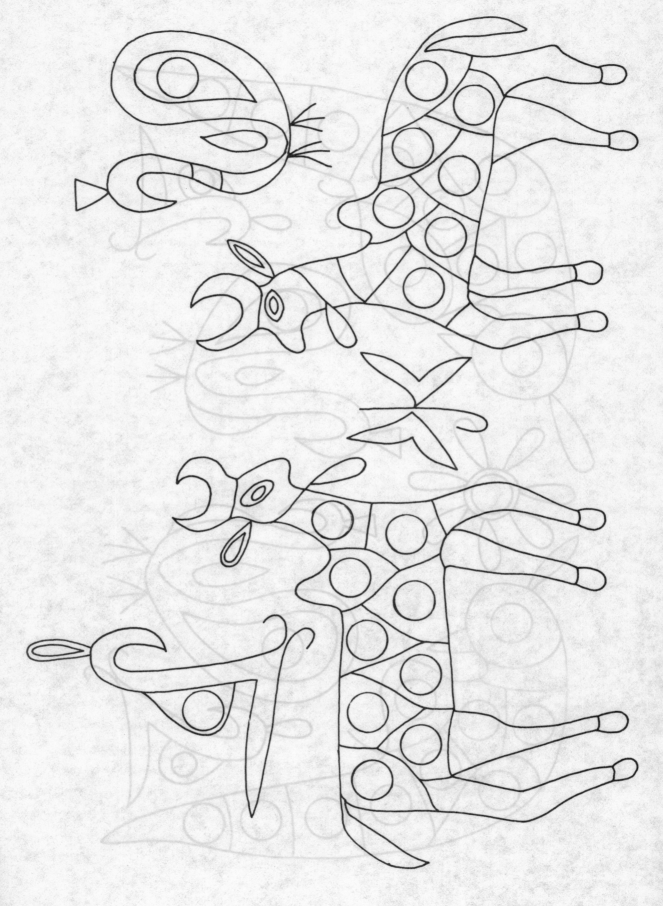

PLATE 8

PLATE 9

PLATE 9

PLATE 10

PLATE 10

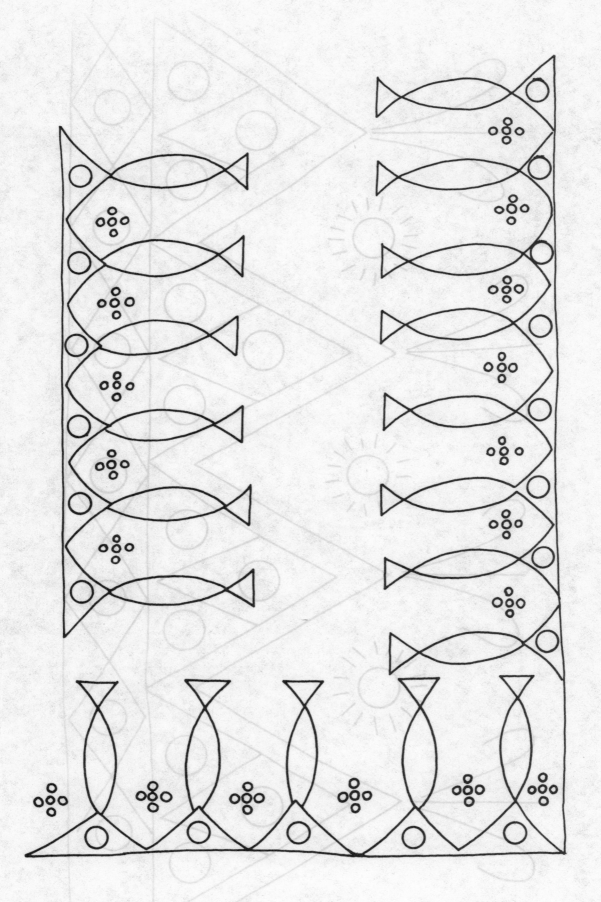

PLATE 11

PLATE II

PLATE 12

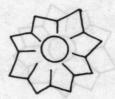

Test Pattern

PLATE 12

Test Pattern

PLATE 13

Test Pattern

PLATE 13

PLATE 14

Test Pattern

PLATE 14

PLATE 15

PLATE 15

PLATE 16

PLATE 16

Test Pattern

PLATE 17

PLATE 17

PLATE 18

PLATE 18

PLATE 19

PLATE 19

PLATE 20

PLATE 20

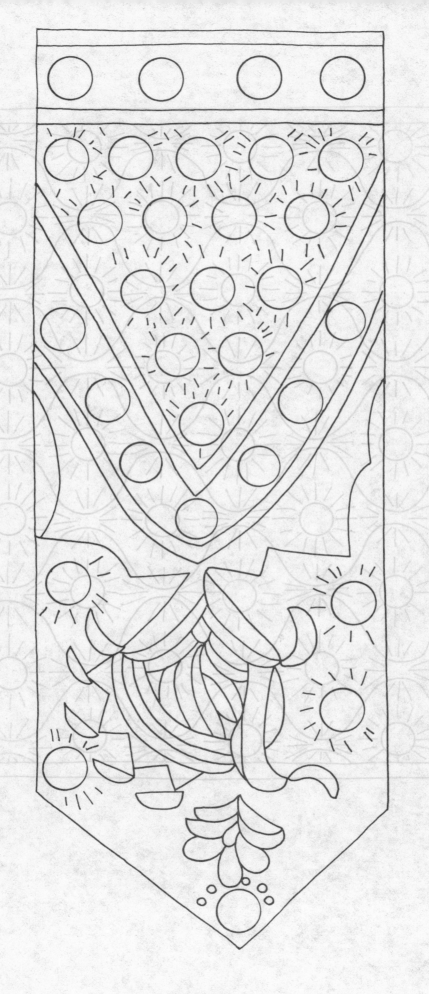

PLATE 21

PLATE 21

PLATE 22

PLATE 22

Test Pattern

PLATE 23

Test Pattern

PLATE 23

PLATE 24

PLATE 24

tightly and carefully. For those projects where ease of care is a prime consideration—such as blouses, tee shirts, pillow covers, linens, etc.—you are well-advised to use the real mirrors. There is no substitute for the authentic touch these handmade discs of silvered glass add to your individually handcrafted piece of embroidery.

For those not concerned with practicality or for those who wish to experiment with shisha work in other techniques and materials, almost anything that is flat and regularly shaped can be anchored to cloth with the stitched framework. Silvery mylar or sheets of colored acetate can be cut into circles, or you can use large sequins. Artificial gems used in jewelry craft can also be attached this way. In remote parts of Afghanistan, ancient coins which are still in circulation are anchored to precious garments with the shisha stitch. By that same token, you can attach pennies, nickels, quarters or silver dollars to the ground material, depending on how much of an investment you are willing to make in the project. Exotic coins from foreign countries impart an even more attractive effect. Antique and unusual buttons which may be picked up in second-hand shops or have been lying at the bottom of your sewing basket make charming substitutes. In a pinch, you can even cut out rounds of cardboard and wrap them in aluminum foil to simulate the shisha, as long as you have no intention of ever washing the finished piece. In fact, none of the above alternatives will withstand washing.

American-made craft mirrors are readily available from local needlework and hobby shops. They come in a wide range of shapes and sizes. Because they are manufactured by a very different process from shisha, they will not stand up to washing or dry cleaning. They are also thicker than shishas and have sharper edges, which makes them more difficult to anchor securely. They do possess the advantages of coming in uniform shapes, sizes and quality, with smooth, unblemished surfaces that reflect light like any normal mirror. Thus, they work nicely in wall hangings and other decorative pieces that are not subjected to everyday wear and tear.

THREADS, NEEDLES AND OTHER ACCESSORIES

Originally, shisha embroidery was worked with fine threads of silk and cotton. The floss was carefully handspun and colored with natural dyes to produce the most lustrous and smooth work. One entire type of Gujarati embroidery is named *heer bharat,* after the precious silk floss called *heer.* Modern shisha work is usually done today with cotton or synthetic rayon thread. Unfortunately, the chemical dyes now used

sometimes make the color combinations seem harsh and garish when compared to the softer tones of the older, naturally processed threads.

For any shisha project you may undertake, a good quality cotton embroidery floss will be perfectly satisfactory. Six-strand embroidery floss, no. 5 or pearl cotton no. 8 are all good choices. Imported Indian silk and cotton embroidery floss can be obtained from some craft dealers, but it is difficult to get and not really worth the trouble. The quality may be uneven at best, and the color, when produced by the use of chemical dyes, is not superior to any domestic floss, and those using natural dyes will run or fade with washing.

Your embroidery needle should be sharp and have a large enough eye so that the floss can pass through without bunching up into separate strands. Embroidery hoops are generally not used in shisha embroidery, but you may feel more comfortable in the beginning if you center the point at which you intend to anchor the mirror in the embroidery hoop, and hold the mirror on to it lightly with your thumb. If that still feels awkward, you can cheat a little and put a tiny drop of white glue on the back of the mirror. This will hold it to the fabric until you have completed the stitched framework. As for other forms of embroidery, you will also need a sharp pair of embroidery scissors, a thimble and a good light.

TRANSFERRING THE DESIGNS

Transferring the designs to your fabric is a fairly simple procedure. Here are directions for using these transfer patterns.

A. Prepare the Fabric: If the fabric is washable, preshrink and remove the sizing by laundering first. Iron carefully to remove all wrinkles. If the fabric ravels badly, it is a good idea to whip the edges by hand with an overcast stitch or to run a large zigzag machine stitch along the edges. Since transfers are made with very high temperatures which might melt synthetic fabrics, use a natural fabric such as cotton or linen. If you are unsure of the fibers in your fabric, test the ironability of the fabric first.

B. Prepare the Ironing Board: To prevent the motif from transferring to your ironing board, place an old sheet or other smooth fabric over the ironing board cover. To obtain a stronger impression of the pattern—especially after the transfer has been used, or on darker fabrics—place a piece of aluminum foil on your board before pressing.

C. Make a Test Transfer: Before beginning any project, it is a good idea to test your iron, the fabric and the evenness of your hand pressure. Cut out one of the motifs marked "Test Pattern" and follow the directions below for making a transfer. If the ink transferred well, you can proceed; if not, adjust either the heat or the length of time.

D. Transfer the Patterns:

1. Use a *dry* iron set at medium or wool.

2. Place the fabric on the ironing board, right side up.

3. Cut out the desired motifs, allowing a margin around the edges of the design. Pin the design to the fabric with the printed side down. Place the pins through the margins to hold the transfer in place on the fabric. Protect the iron by placing a sheet of tissue paper between the transfer and the iron.

4. Place the heated iron on the transfer and hold down for about 5 seconds. Apply a firm, downward even pressure to all parts of the design, being especially careful to get the outer edges, such as the tips of leaves and flowers. Do not move the iron back and forth across the fabric as this will cause the transfer pattern to blur. After the transfer has been used once, add 2-3 seconds for each additional transfer.

5. Carefully remove one pin and lift one side of the transfer paper to see whether the complete design is indicated on the fabric. If not, replace the pin and repeat the process, concentrating on the area that did not transfer. Do not remove all the pins until you are sure the design has been successfully transferred. Once the pattern has been unpinned it is almost impossible to register it to the fabric again.

6. When you are satisfied that the transferring has been completed, unpin the transfer paper and peel it off. You will want to save the transfer paper to use for additional repeats (you can usually get four or more transfers from each pattern) or to use as a check on the design. If the design is not clear enough, you can refer to the transfer sheet and reinforce vague areas on the fabric with a waterproof felt pen or laundry marker. Make sure that the ink is completely waterproof because just the moisture from a steam iron can cause the ink to run and ruin your embroidery.

E. Special Instructions for Use on Dark Fabrics: If you wish to use these patterns on dark fabric on which transfer ink will not show up, or if you need additional repeats of the same transfer, put a piece of tracing paper over the uninked side of the transfer and trace the design. Discard the original transfer paper and pin the tracing in place on the fabric. Slip a piece of dressmaker's carbon, color-side down, between the fabric and the tracing; do not pin the carbon. With a hard, even pressure, trace a few lines with a tracing wheel, stylus or similar tool. Raise one corner of the tracing and the carbon to check the impression. If the results are too faint, apply more pressure; if too heavy, less pressure. After adjusting the impression, trace the entire design and then remove the carbon and carefully remove one pin to see whether the design is intact on the fabric *before removing the pattern.*

IMPORTANT

Since these transfer patterns are made to be used more than once, the ink will not readily wash out of the fabric. It is therefore important that the embroidery cover all transfer markings.

ATTACHING THE MIRRORS TO THE FABRIC

Step. 1. Align the center of the mirror with the center of the circle in the transfer pattern and place the mirror against the fabric. Do not be concerned if the mirror is larger than the circle; this is done on purpose. If the circle of the transfer pattern is larger than the size mirror you happen to be using, don't worry; the framework of stitches will hide any outlines.

Step 2. Mark or imagine four points around the outside of the mirror, as close as possible to its edges, to form a square. Bring the needle up from the back of the material at point A.

Step 3. Bring the thread down across the right hand surface of the mirror and push the needle through to the back of the material at point B.

Step 4. Catch a small stitch at point B and bring the needle up next to it in the direction away from the mirror, to the right. Bring the thread across the lower surface of the mirror and insert it at point C. Catch a stitch and bring it up slightly below the point.

Step 5. Bring the thread up across the left side of the mirror and insert the needle at point D. Catch a stitch, this time directly to the left of this point and bring the needle up.

Step 6. Bring the thread over across the top of the mirror, back to point A. The thread should then be anchored securely to the back.

Step 7. (Optional) If a stronger mesh is desired, give the whole stitched square a 45° turn and work a second square of stitches between the first.

Step 8. Once the mirror is anchored to the fabric, a buttonhole stitch is worked around the entire circle. Bring the needle up at point C. Keeping the thread flush to the fabric and to the right, bring the needle back towards you, catching underneath the meshwork.

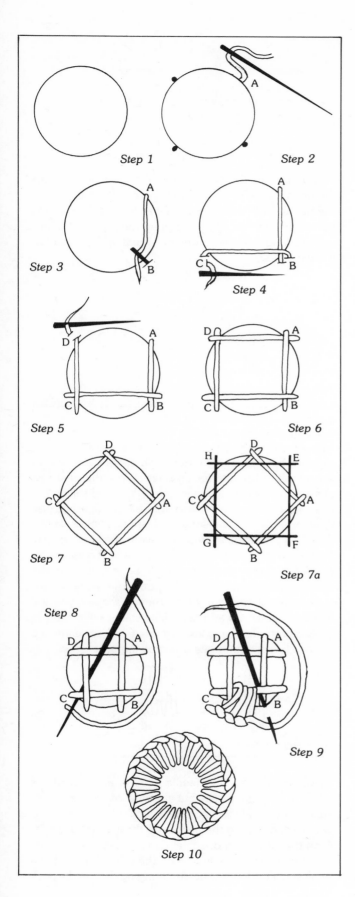

Step 1

Step 2

Step 3

Step 4

Step 5

Step 6

Step 7

Step 7a

Step 8

Step 9

Step 10

Step 9. Insert the needle into the fabric as close to the mirror's edge as possible. Take a small stitch, making sure the loose thread from the previous stitch remains beneath the point of the needle. Pull the thread gently yet firmly.

Step 10. Keep working around the mirror, the direction of the stitches always radiating outward, away from the center. Proceed counterclockwise until the starting point is reached.

OTHER DECORATIVE AND FILLING STITCHES

Running: The first stitch that most people learn in sewing is the running stitch, an evenly spaced in-and-out line from right to left, good for joining seams. In embroidery it is most used as a base for other stitches, to define and hold a line, or to pad an area to be covered with heavier stitching.

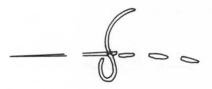

Backstitch: Bring the needle up through the fabric at *A* (one finished-stitch length from the beginning of the line) and insert the needle at *B* (on the beginning of the line). Bring it up again at *C* (one stitch-length to the left of *A*). The needle will always be inserted at the end of the preceding stitch.

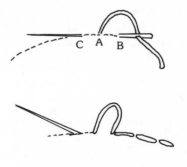

Stem or Outline: This stitch is worked from left to right but the needle is put into the fabric from right to left. Bring the needle up through the fabric at *A,* put it in again at *B* (this is the length of the stitch as it appears on the surface of the fabric). Bring the needle out again almost half way back to A at C. Put it in again at D (the same stitch length from C as the A-B length) and bring it out almost back to B. The needle as it goes under the fabric can slant very slightly. The thread must always be kept to the same side of the needle, below for stem and above for outline.

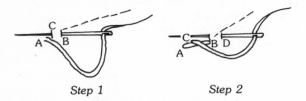

Step 1   *Step 2*

Chain: Bring the needle up through the fabric at A. With the left thumb, hold the thread in a loop on the surface of the fabric, inserting the needle again at A and bringing it out at B through the loop. Pull the thread gently and not too tightly to the left, hold another loop and insert the needle at B again. The loops should never be pulled into a straight line but should be softly rounded in appearance.

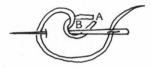

Open Chain: Made the same way as Chain Stitch, but the needle is inserted at a slant to form broad, open loops. Bring the thread up at A; pull through. Make a loop with the thread down and around to the right, holding the loop down with the thumb. Insert needle at B and bring diagonally to C; bring up at C and pull through loop loosely. Make a loop down and around to right. With the point of the needle, drag first loop over to line at D, then insert needle (inside first loop); bring up at E and pull through loosely. Keep loops loose.

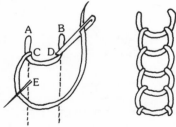

Lazy Daisy: This is a single chain stitch, often used as a small flower petal or leaf. The thread is brought over the end of the loop and the needle inserted at C, about one thread beyond B, to hold the loop in place.

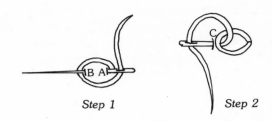

Step 1   *Step 2*

Satin: Bring the thread up at A; pull through. Insert the needle at B, bring out at C and pull through. Insert the needle at D, very close to B, and bring up at E. Do not crowd stitches. Do not pull up too tightly. Continue following the design outline, holding the thread in parallel lines.

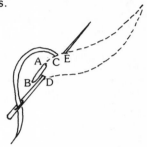

Long-and-Short Satin: If an area is too broad for satin stitch, long-and-short should be used. Work as for satin but with *every other* stitch about two-thirds of the length of the alternating ones. Work the next row in stitches of all the same length. (They will still be uneven in appearance on the unfinished edge because they must touch the long and short stitches above them). If the fabric is loosely woven, the stitches may create a small hole where the ends meet. To avoid this and keep a smooth surface, work all the way into the ends of the stitches in the previous row. As you progress to fan shapes and other uneven shapes, you will find it necessary to add extra little stitches like wedges to accommodate a widening area, or to eliminate stitches to accommodate a narrowing area.

Step 1   *Step 2*

Herringbone: The needle goes in and out of the fabric from right to left but the line of stitching progresses from left to right. It is worked between two parallel lines. Bring the needle up through the fabric at A on the left end of one line, carry it diagonally across to the right and put it in at B on the other line, taking a small stitch under the line and bringing the needle back out at *C*. Cross diagonally to the right to the other line and take another stitch from *D* to *E*. Continue back and forth between the lines, being sure to keep the angles the same and the stitch lengths even.

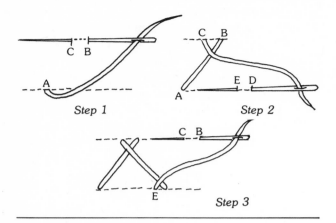

Step 1

Step 2

Step 3

Closed Herringbone: Herringbone stitch worked closer together. On the wrong side this stitch forms two rows of backstitch.

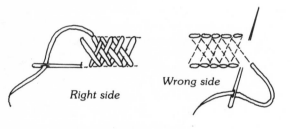

Right side

Wrong side

Interlacing: Work a large herringbone, making sure that the thread is slipped under after working each top stitch. With a second thread, weave in a counter-clockwise direction. (The second thread does not pierce the fabric.) At the end, reverse the direction and continue weaving the lower and center crosses.

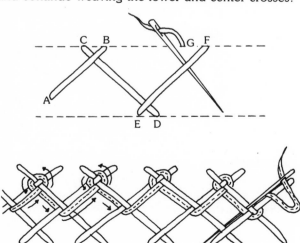

French Knots: Bring the needle up through the fabric at *A* and pull the thread up firmly. With the left hand wrap the thread around the needle from the eye end toward the point end, one, two, or three times. Insert the needle into the fabric at *B* (about one thread away from *A*). Let all the wraps of thread slide down the needle so that they are close to the fabric, and pull the needle to the wrong side, securing the knot of thread against the surface. For practice, start with one wrap and work up to the larger numbers.

Step 1

Step 2

Couching (Laid Work): This stitch is generally used for holding down a line of heavier thread with stitches of a lighter one. Bring the heavy thread up through the fabric at the beginning of the line and hold it along the line with the left hand. With a finer thread take small stitches across the heavy thread at distances of from ¼″ to ½″. Conceal the end of the heavy thread by pulling it back through the fabric to the wrong side.

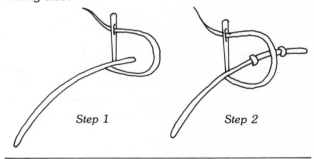

Step 1

Step 2

Cross: Composed of two straight stitches which overlap at the midpoints to form a cross shape. May be worked alone, in a row, or close together with ends touching.

Maltese Cross: Starting at *A*, work foundation stitches, following the arrows and the letters. The needle pierces the fabric only at the points indicated by letters. Then weave another thread (often a contrasting color) in the direction of the arrows, until all of the crosses are woven. Another journey of lacing, following the same pattern, may be worked. Another variation is to work the second journey so that the weaving is accomplished *over* where the thread went *under* on the first journey, etc.

Buttonhole or Blanket: Bring thread up at *A;* pull through. Make a loop to the left of the line and down and around to the right. Insert needle at *B;* bring out at *C* (just inside of line to be covered). With loop beneath needle, pull through. Make a loop down and around to the right. Insert needle at *D* and bring out at *E.* With loop beneath needle, pull through. Note that *C* and *E* do not come quite to the line to be covered. Continue to the end of the line. (The stitches may also be placed so closely together that no fabric shows between.)

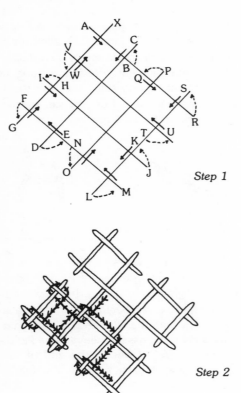

Step 1

Step 2

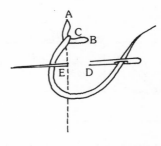

Ladder: This is actually a combination of a reverse chain stitch on each side and a straight stitch between. Although the stitch looks complicated, it is not difficult.

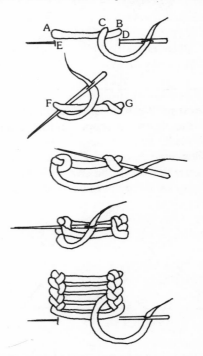

Seeding: The seed stitch is a delicate filling stitch, which must be worked in relatively heavy thread and spaced evenly to be effective. It is a short straight stitch, always worked in groups at many angles, just as scattered seed would fall; hence the name.

Notes on the Plates

Plates 1-15 are adaptations from an *ochhad*, a large wall hanging from Kathiawar, probably executed by *Mochi* embroiderers. The hanging depicts the major battle scene from the great Indian epic poem, *The Mahabharata*. Two mythic clans of ancient India, the *Pandavas* and the *Kauravas*, the personifications of good and evil, fight a pitched battle for supremacy. The *Pandavas* emerge victorious and learn many ethical and religious lessons in the process. The embroidery is worked in cotton floss on a natural, handwoven ground. Fine chain stitch is used for the outlines and line details. Larger areas are filled with satin stitch and closed herringbone stitches. The entire hanging is surrounded by a series of borders which have been embroidered separately and appliqued on to the finished piece.

Plate 1: Archer mounted on an elephant. The large areas around the mirrors are filled with satin stitch in various colors; legs are filled with closed herringbone. Chain stitch outline is worked in black. The tiny eye slit is blank.

Plate 2: Archer mounted on a horse. Worked in the same way as the elephant and rider, except the outline is in maroon. There is a similar motif of a camel and archer, with the camel looking exactly like the horse save for a slight hump behind an elongated neck.

Plate 3: Two brothers from the *Pandava* clan, heroes of the epic battle. The design is outlined in chain stitch with the filling a combination of multicolored closed herringbone and satin stitch.

Plate 4: Lunbar motif showing the crescent moon with central mirrors representing moonlight. Borders are done in chain stitch with a single row of closed herringbone for filling. The moon is flanked by two whimsical parakeets worked in the same fashion.

Plate 5: Lunar motif showing the full moon. The outer ring is worked in chain stitch filled with closed herringbone. Space between the central mirrors is open.

Plate 6: Two women performing some ritual or everyday chore. They may be churning butter,

Plates 1–15

which is an act of religious significance as well as a necessary part of pastoral life. The figures are outlined in chain stitches with herringbone and satin filling.

Plate 7: Ceremonial chariot drawn by bullock. The figures are outlined in chain stitch. Closed herringbone is used to fill narrower areas, and satin stitch is the filling for the wider areas around the mirrors on the bullock's body.

Plate 8: Decorative pastoral motif. Two bullocks are flanked by a peacock on the left and a parakeet on the right. A butterfly hovers between the two beasts.

Plate 9: Two large parrots surrounding a pair of peacocks and parakeets. The bird, an ever-present decorative motif so characteristic of Gujarati shisha work, is considered a symbol of long life, happiness and romance. What is so endearing about the renderings is the fact that such an abstract depiction can capture and convey the lively essence of these creatures through the bold use of shape and color. The solid area of different colors on the parrots—yellow, purple, gray, green—contrast with the more stately colors used in the peacocks and the duller ones used for the parakeets. The parrots are outlined in black chain stitch, the peacocks in orange and the parakeets in red. The large sections of the parrot are filled with satin stitch; the peacock and parakeet with closed herringbone. An abstract flower is at the center.

Plate 10: Characteristic border of pyramids. Three is considered a magical number, and pyramids, triangles and triads abound in shisha embroidery. Three lines emanating from the peak of a pyramid and the three sections of mirrors which fill it reinforce the magical qualities. Outlines are in chain stitch. The outside border of the pyramids is worked in closed herringbone filling, the sections in satin stitch. Underneath is another border. The diamonds are worked in satin stitch around the mirrors and the triangles are empty.

Plate 11: Another border design showing how the corners are worked. The crosses are actually four single chain stitches, but Frenchknos would also be attractive. The convex shapes are outlines in chain stitch and filled with closed herringbone.

Plates 12 and 13: The central moif of the solar disc. A mirror forms the focus about which the arms of the sun's rays rotate. Numerous mirrors are interspersed to give the impression of light. The circles are filled in closed herringbone, while the arms are done in satin stitch. The space between the arms is left bare. The pyramids are filled with satin stitch; the rays from the top are worked in chain.

Plate 14: Smaller solar disc. This is worked in the same style as the preceding plate.

Plate 15: Main appliquéd border motifs of abstract flowers and idealized cows' heads. These motifs are worked entirely in chain stitch on a black cotton ground. The cows are outlined in red chain stitch filled with rows of white, green and yellow chain stitch. The flowers are predominantly white, with red and green details. The border itself is outlined by a single row of yellow chain stitch. After completion it was appliquéd to the main piece and thin borders of orange, green and red trim added to the edge.

Plates 16, 17

A *sthapan*, a wall hanging depicting a scene from Hindu mythology, worked by nomadic *Kanbi* embroiderers of Gujarat, is the source for Plates 16 and 17. This hanging narrates the popular *Rosa Lila* dance of the god Krishna and his devotees, the milkmaids or *gopis*. The god was said to be so handsome and entrancing that all human beings were drawn to him. One day he was dancing in a clearing and all the young women of the village abandoned their tasks and joined him in a large circle. Since he could not dance with each woman at once, with his great powers, he cast an illusion over each maiden so she thought that Krishna was dancing with her and her alone. This allegory makes the point that we are all like those *gopis* before God, desiring to be united with him in our hearts. The *Rosa Lila* is a popular folk dance which is widely performed in Gujarat. This work is done on an orange ground of hand-dyed and handwoven cotton. The figures are not outlined but are worked in closed herringbone and dense satin stitch. Line details are done in chain stitch. There is an outer border of pyramids and an inner one of mirrors. The two borders are separated by a band of couched gold metallic thread. A second such band sets the borders off from the main piece. The colors of green, brown, purple and magenta proivde a rich, warm feeling against the orange background, which makes the moral of this story all the more affecting.

Plate 16: The god Krishna dancing at the center of the circle. The sense of movement is conveyed dramatically with the outward-spread hands and arms, the extended feet and billowing garments of the highly abstract figure. The narrow bands are worked in satin stitch while the larger interior areas around the mirrors are empty.

Plate 17: One of the *gopis*, dancing with her face towards the god. Her arms are outstretched towards him as she whirls around in bliss. The bands of the skirt are worked in different colors in closed herringbone and the torso is embroidered in bands of satin stitch.

Plate 18: Border motifs. The border on the left contains stylized flowers outlined in white backstitch; the petals are filled with areas of purple, green and yellow closed herringbone. The border on the right is also filled with floral designs. The petals are outlined in white backstitch, while the space inside the petals is left unadorned. The areas surrounding the flowers are filled in satin stitch. Bands of narrow herringbone stitch enclose both borders.

Plate 19

An *aba,* a long tunic worn over baggy trousers by women, is the source for Plate 19. This *aba* is from Kuch. The material is handloomed maroon cotton, with an overall embroidered design of mirrors interspread with Maltese crosses and squares worked in interlacing stitch in green, orange, blue and white. Unusually, the mirrors are set in tear-dropped shaped cross patterns and outlined in white backstitch. The embroidery on the front and back yokes of the *aba* have been embroidered separately and stitched on. This is often done to preserve an old and beautiful piece of embroidery when the garment to which it is attached is no longer wearable.

Plate 19: Motifs from the front yoke of the blouse. Rows of embroidery are divided by a line of yellow chain stitch. The mirrors are enclosed in circles of blanket stitch and herringbone with empty space between that and the outer rings of intertwining chain stitch. Thin bands of widely spaced herringbone stitch

Plate 18

Plate 18 is derived from a *chakla,* a bridal wall hanging from Kuch, worked by *Lohana* embroiderers. The piece has three borders with main motifs of characteristic many-sided geometric figures. The squares are worked in alternating sections of satin stitch, closed herringbone, and interlacing stitch. A row of mirrors divides the motifs. The cotton ground is indigo and the cotton floss is purple, yellow, white, muted green and gray.

in blue, with a single white couching stitch in the middle, intervene. Narrow bands with a wavy row of yellow chain stitch down the center are filled on either side by solid colors worked in satin stitch with the middle stitch couched with white thread. The effect of the entire motif is at once striking and sophisticated.

Plate 20

Plate 20 derives from a *thela,* a shoulderbag from Gujarat. This is a modern piece, done primarily for the tourist trade. The ground is bright green cotton with embroidery in red, white and yellow.

Plate 20: Front decorative panel. this is worked in chain stitch and lazy daisy surrounding the mirrors. The points at which the wavy rows of chain stitch meet are also accentuated by lazy daisy stitches. Some areas are filled with closed herringbone. The outer border is filled with herringbone and enclosed by single rows of chain stitch.

Plates 21, 22 and 23 are adapted from two *bokhanis,* men's wedding scarfs from Sindh, Tharparkar region. The scarfs are made of two long strips of cotton cloth joined together along the narrow end. Teh two free ends of the pieces are finished with beadwork and cotton tassels. Narrow borders separate sections of differing geometric motifs. The irregular size and shape of the shishas on the piece on the left indicate that this is an older work, perhaps from the beginning of the 20th century. The small regularly shaped mirrors on the piece on the right indicate it is of more recent manufacture. This later piece clearly shows the characteristic Sindhi combination of shisha embroidery with counted thread designs.

Plate 21: A section of the earlier wedding scarf. This contains a very complex pattern which begins with an inner pyramid of mirrors with interspersed seed stitches and French knots. It is enclosed by a border of laid work outlined on both sides by stem stitch. The outer chevron of mirrors is filled with shisha alternating with Maltese crosses. This is bordered by another band of laid work. The entire pyramid is topped by a crown of interlacing stitches out of which blooms a large, irregular *buta* executed in ladder stitch. Above that is a smaller *buti* and shisha surrounded by seed stitches. The description may make the piece sound somewhat overpowering and cluttered, but the combination of geometric and stylized floral motifs is worked with typically Sindhi finesse and understatment.

Plate 22: A section of the later wedding scarf. Two pyramids of mirrors point towards a central cluster of flowers, surrounded by leaves and smaller buds. The chevrons of mirrors enclose flowers with petals filled with ladder stitch, outlined in open chain stitch. Stem stitch outlines the strips of ladder stitch. The inner triangles of the crown are filled with satin stitch. Stem stitch separates them from the outer zigzag of ladder stitch. Characteristically, the larger motifs are all outlined in small, white running stitch.

Plate 23: Another section of the later scarf showing the intergration of floral and geometric motifs. The borders and dividing bands of leaves and boxes are worked in ladder stitch edged in the typical black stem stitch, as are the star-like flower and leaves which alternate with the shisha in the outer borders. The central mirror is ringed wiht a concentric circle of buttonhole stitch. The square is divided into nine boxes, three times three, a most auspicious number for a wedding garment.

Plate 24

Plate 24 comes from a *kurta,* an embroidered piece of cloth to be sewn into a blouse from Quetta, Baluchistan in Pakistan. This is a modern piece, done for the export and tourist trade, of bright red cotton ground worked in cotton floss. The quality of the work in this modern piece is regrettably much inferior to the older pieces. The stitches are hurried and loosely executed; the chemical colors are harsh and the color schemes not well thought out. The overall effect, however, is generally pleasing, and the embroidery would look quite handsome when attached to the yoke of a blouse or long dress.

Plate 24: The major motif of the flowers outlined in long backstitch. The petals are filled with yellow satin stitch. The mirrors are interspersed with lazy daisy stitches in white and occasional cross stitches. The border is also outlined in long backstitch, and the hourglass shapes are filled with yellow and green satin stitches. The diamonds are filled with a single white cross stitch, couched at the center with a single stitch.

Plates 22, 23

Plate 21

Mail-Order Suppliers

Mirrors and other materials needed for shisha embroidery are now available in an increasing number of needlework shops; check with your local needlework, craft or hobby shop. If they do not have what you need in stock, they may be glad to order it for you.

If, however, you are unable to find a source in your area, the following mail-order suppliers may be able to help you. Be sure to enclose a stamped, self-addressed envelope along with your inquiry. This will insure a prompt reply and the gratitude of the busy suppliers as well.

Aardvark Adventures, P.O. Box 2449, Livermore, CA 94550. *Indian mirrors in 10mm, 19mm, 25mm, 30mm in rounds in standard antique finish, "perfect" finish, plus colors. Also squares and triangles. Wide assortment of books, textile and craft supplies listed in catalog. Copy available for $1.00. Wholesale inquiries welcome.*

Bazaar Del Mundo, Yarn and Yardage Shops, 2754 Calhoun Street, San Diego, CA 92110. *Indian mirrors in gold, blue, green and silver in 1/2" and 1" diameters.*

Berger Specialty Company, 413 East 8th Street, Los Angeles, CA 90014. *Indian mirrors in 1/2" and larger diameters; wooden and metal beads, spangles, sequins and other decorative jewelry findings.*

Bhavneeta Novelties, 245 Euston Road, London, N.W. 1, England. *Indian mirrors in assorted sizes.*

Chaparral, 3733 Westheimer Road, Suite 7, Houston, TX 77027. *Indian mirrors in assorted sizes, shapes and colors.*

Elliot, Greene and Company, Inc., 37 West 37th Street, New York, NY 10018. *Extensive assortment of spangles, sequins, and mirrored decorations in a wide range of sizes, shapes and styles; beads made of glass, wood, metal, plastic; motif/appliqués made of sequins, beads or rhinestones.*

Emporium de Perles de Montreal, Inc., 364 Victoria Avenue, Montreal, Canada H3Z 2N4. *Indian mirrors in assorted shapes and sizes; beads, sequins and spangles from all over the world.*

Eye of the Needle, Vintage 1870, Yountville, CA 94599. *Indian mirrors in assorted sizes and ⌐hapes.*

It's a Stitch, 4446½ Forman Avenue, Toluca Lake, CA 91602. *Indian mirrors in assorted sizes.*

Kitsophrenia, Inc., P.O. Box 5042, Glendale, CA 91201. *Indian mirrors in assorted shapes and sizes; imported Indian metal spangles and metal-framed mirrors; patterns and kits for shisha work belts, bags and other projects.*

Vima, S.P.A., 2727 Marconi Avenue, Sacramento, CA 95821. *Indian mirrors in assorted sizes. Catalog available for $2. Wholesale inquiries welcome.*